Copyright © 2023 Joan Enockson

All rights reserved. This book, or any parts, may not be reproduced in any form without written permission from the publisher.

"Counting Christmas Kittens" is a work of nonfiction. This educational book is original, and all graphics were obtained using the software program, Canva, while maintaining a pro subscription license. Therefore, all graphics may be used for commercial use.

ISBN: 978-1-958023-31-0 (Hardcover)
ISBN: 978-1-958023-32-7 (Paperback)
ISBN: 978-1-958023-33-4 (ePub)

Written by: Joan Enockson
Graphic Designer: Joan Enockson

First printing, 2023

Tall Girl Publishing
Laurens, IA

tallgirlpublishing.com

Dedication

This book is dedicated to all who have adopted kittens and cats from the Humane Society. Pictured below is my fur grandfeline, Hemmingway, who was adopted by my son, Lucas, and his wife, Morgan.

Counting Christmas Kittens

Written and Graphic Designed by:
Joan Enockson

This book belongs to:

_____

A gift from:

_____

Two kittens,

Four.

Five kittens,

Seven kittens more.

Eight kittens,

Nine kittens,

Ten under the tree.

How many kittens can you count on Christmas Day?

You did it! Great job!

Tall Girl Publishing

Ages 1-4

 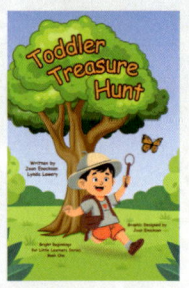 

Ages 8-12

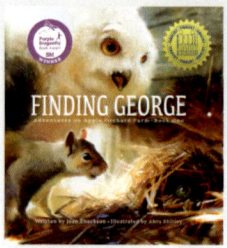 

Ages 4-8

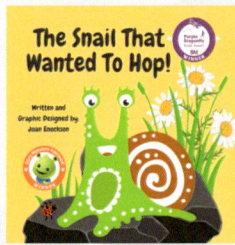 

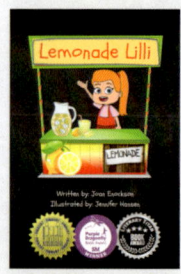 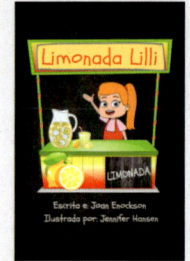

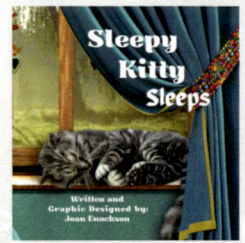 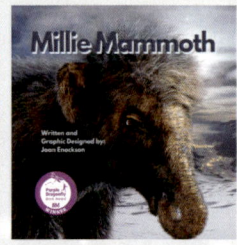 

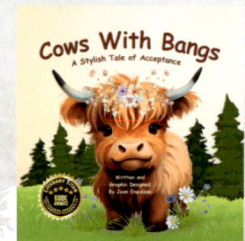 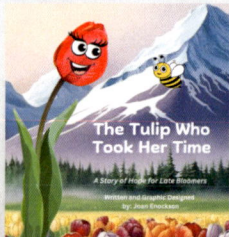 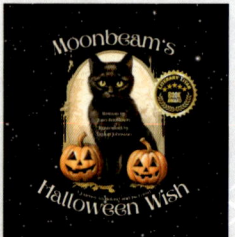

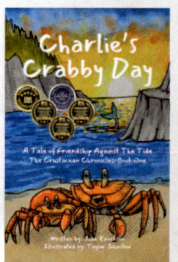  

About the Author

Joan Enockson blends her passion for education, music, and writing to create captivating children's books. With a deep understanding of children's social-emotional needs, she weaves stories that touch on friendship, problem-solving, citizenship, and patriotism.

Having spent years teaching children of various ages in the public school system, Joan's experiences have shaped her writing style, allowing her to engage and intrigue young readers. She knows how to captivate their imaginations while incorporating important life lessons that support 21st Century skills.

www.tallgirlpublishing.com

Laurens, IA

Tall Girl Publishing

www.ingramcontent.com/pod-product-compliance
Lightning Source LLC
Chambersburg PA
CBRC091204010526
44107CB00021B/1238